A GARMENT of GRACE

Dennis Tinsman

Faith, Hope, & Love Publishing
P.O. Box 775
Nashville, MI 49073-0775

Library of Congress Catalog Card No. 91-92863

ISBN 0-9643411-1-5 (paperback)

2 3 4 5 6 Printing / Year 99 98 97 96 95

Printed in the United States of America

Contents

Preface: The Shepherd's Love

Dennis! Hey, Dennis! Over here! I'm over here! Come on, boy! Remember the last time you wandered over by the tall green grass. Stay where you can see and hear me.

Baa! Baa! Oh dear, look at you! Just look at you! You're a bloody mess! You've been mauled by that wolf again. This makes about eight times you've wandered away. I have had enough of your stubborn and disobedient spirit. The rest of my flock doesn't behave like this. Don't you understand I want you right here beside me, where you can grow up and learn to value my friendship and your walk with me? I'm going to do something to you that I don't do very often. I am a Good Shepherd and I love my sheep. Because I love you, I'm going to break your leg. I will carry you over my shoulder until it heals. You will feel pain for a long time, but you will learn to stay with me. As I carry you close, I will talk with you. The only voice you will hear is mine. When your leg begins to heal, I will put you with the flock so you can limp around. Your limp and the pain you feel will serve as a reminder of how much I love you and want you next to me. When your leg heals, you will tell the rest of my sheep what happened. They will learn from your pain.

Acknowledgments

Being a few months shy of thirty-eight, I had found myself at the end of the long, winding road of inconsistency. I had nowhere else to turn except back to God. The following stories are true and reveal the grace, forgiveness, and restoring power I found through faith in Jesus Christ. *A Garment of Grace* is the result of a long-suffering God. I have devoted the rest of my life to sharing with and reaching out to others for the cause of Christ.

I didn't start writing to become a writer. I started writing to empty out the trash inside me. I shared the waste material of my innermost self with a fifty-two-year-old preacher who had never done anything remotely like I had. Actually, that's not entirely so. There was one thing that we share—that we both had in common. That one thing saved my life. There was also an eighty-three-year-old lady who shared the same thing and became my adopted grandmother. She is almost blind in sight, but with her simplicity and wisdom, she could see all the way to eternity. It was in and through these two godly individuals that I would come to know my self-worth in Jesus Christ. They would succeed where everything and everyone else had failed. They would succeed because they were acting as ambassadors for Jesus Christ, and he never fails.

I wish to dedicate *A Garment of Grace* to Mrs. Leola Bivens, known to me as Grandma, and Pastor Lester DeGroot, along with the congregation of Nashville Baptist Church in Nashville, Michigan.

Chapter 1
Keep the Corral Clean

I stood almost knee-deep in what horse ranchers call slop. It's what you get when you mix mud, manure, and a few days of rain. The mixture is messy, smelly, and certainly not conducive to the comfort of most big-city suit-and-tie folk.

I was standing right in the middle of it, literally! The ranch I was working on is about fifteen miles outside of Battle Creek, Michigan. Standing in this mess made by nature, I looked just outside the feeding corral. The landscape was beautiful, with rolling hills of uncut alfalfa, corn, and green pastures separated by man-made partitions called fences. The autumn leaves were changing, and to a city boy from Seattle it looked magnificent.

Now there is a certain way to get manure into a wheelbarrow without clearing the entire corral of all its soil and leaving a big pit. You need a pitchfork, and you probe four to eight inches at each scoop. The manure stays on the pitchfork and the good soil and water run through.

While absolutely engrossed in this necessary task, I leaned on an electric fence while standing in wet soupy manure and holding in my hand a pitchfork that was sticking into the ground.

As I was recovering from the shock, one of the mares came up to me. She's a beauty. I nicknamed her Black Beauty.

I scratched her neck and ears. Tears began to run down my cheeks. I began thinking of the series of events

1

in my life that had brought me to this ranch in Michigan. I thought about the drugs and alcohol that had ruined my relationship with my Lord and my family. I thought about my wife and two small kids, who loved me but could stand for no more. I thought about my willful disobedience toward God; the lying and deceiving.

My life had become just like the corral. The waste material of a life of sin had built up. The rains came and made it a soupy mess. Resentments had packed the hate like horse hoofs on manure, and only one word could describe what my life had turned into—*defiance*. Defiance toward God and Christian precepts. It started with a little beer here and a little marijuana there. Then crack cocaine came into the picture. Day by day, week by week, month by month, the deterioration of a man loved by God, with an eagerness for ministry, became a corral of bitterness.

Nobody liked me! Everybody had a grudge against me! Friends and employers were to blame!

Yes, standing in the middle of that soupy mess, I was showed by God what I had offered friends, family, employers, and, worst of all, *him!*

I felt an uncontrollable, overwhelming peace. God was showing me the real problem: *me!*

I had given my life to Jesus years earlier, but I don't believe there had ever been a time when I surrendered all. I would make my own plans and put God's stamp of approval on them. My life had gone from one crisis to another. The power of self-will had been running rampant in my life for years. And like Black Beauty, Jesus was waiting just outside to spend time with me. That's True Love. That is Real Grace. A God who still loved me—and who had died for me—had been waiting all these years. He was willing to take on the task of cleaning out my corral.

2

I recall a hymn I first heard at a Billy Graham crusade, as a boy. "Just as I am and waiting not, / To rid my soul of one dark blot. / To Thee Whose blood can cleanse each spot, / O Lamb of God I come, I come." The parable of the prodigal son raced through my mind. "This son of mine was lost and has come home."

It's true in my life and the lives of others since the beginning of time—complete submission to God through faith in Jesus Christ is the only answer to real peace and a life of true harmony with God.

My thoughts turned to the apostle Paul. I recall him asking God to take away the thorn in his side. Some theologians believe his bad eyesight was his thorn in the side. I believe it could have been the memory of his persecution of Stephen. For me, my thorn in the side is the terrible things I did that affected my family and other people. God uses these memories to remind me of where I am now. It is through God's grace, through faith in Jesus Christ, that I can face all the tomorrows. I don't know what the future will bring, or if my family will ever trust me again. Today I am able to accept God's plans for me. I hear him say quite frequently, "My Grace is Sufficient."

I finished cleaning the corral later that day. You couldn't even tell it was the same place. Fresh dirt had not been added, just a lot of hard work separating the manure from the dirt. Once the manure was gone, the rain seeped into the ground and there were no more puddles. With dedication to each scoop of slop, and a commitment to persevere the stench of manure as it was removed from a place it didn't belong, the corral was *fit* for a stallion . . . a champion; God's champion. If you have manure in your life, I wish to share a few encouragements.

3

1. Confess it and ask God to reveal all sin in your life. He will.
2. Be honest with God. He knows all about you anyway.
3. Share it with a friend who has had a consistent walk with Jesus.
4. Spend much time in his word getting to know Jesus.
5. Keep pitchforking the manure. This task is not finished until we are with Jesus in Heaven.

KEEP THE CORRAL CLEAN

Chapter 2

Pastor

Have you ever met someone that was so unique that you couldn't say, "He reminds me of . . . of . . . whoever"? Everyone called him Pastor. Not Pastor this or Pastor that, just Pastor. He was short and stocky, and he would peer over the top of his glasses when he was angry or trying to make a point. My first one-on-one with him, he was doing just that, peering over the top of his glasses as he leaned back in his chair and proceeded to blast me with what I know today as the Truth. I couldn't seem to make my point with him. However, he sure made his point with me. He devastated me with the question, "If three treatment centers, numerous counselors, and preachers couldn't help you, what makes you think a simple country preacher like myself can?" I was speechless. I had gone to him to win my wife back. He proceeded to tell me I didn't deserve her back, and that I should be more concerned with my relationship with my Lord than my relationship with my wife.

I believe the only reason he bothered with me after that first meeting was because I was honest with him. He asked me how old I was. I told him thirty-seven. He said "Thirty-seven, huh! You have enough trash in your life for three men of eighty years old." He told me that I reminded him of an old car he once had. He said it had been hit real hard. After the car was fixed it never did go down the road properly. It kind of tracked sideways. He said, "And that was after being hit once. You've been hit at least seven or

5

eight times that way. You're not going to run down the road straight. Your frame's crooked. You look good, but you run down the road crooked." I thought, *Marvelous! Is this Dutchman telling me that I'm—unrepairable; that there is no hope? This guy sure doesn't sound like any Baptist preacher I've ever heard.*

I had been a car salesman for many years. That attitude of selling *today* and making a sale *today* did little to help me learn patience. When I asked him, "How long will it take to get me the way God wants me?" he replied with this: "It took Moses forty years! How long is it going to take you?" He then looked at me and started laughing. "Open your Bible," he said, "and turn to Psalm Fifty-five."

Pastor then took out a sheet of paper and started writing. On that sheet of paper was my first assignment. On it was written: *"Psalm fifty-five—When the rug has been pulled out!"* It was underlined and looked like a prescription, with the scribbling and church heading on the paper. He then said, "Dennis, read Psalm Fifty-five out loud to me!" So I did. The content of Psalm Fifty-five was no doubt about David crying out when the carpet had been pulled out. I could barely get the words out. When I was finished, Pastor said, "Let me see your assignment. I also want you to read these verses in Proverbs." On the paper he wrote, "Proverbs 23:29–35." "Now, Dennis" —he spoke harshly— "make a list of what will happen to you if you ever drink or take cocaine again, based on your past history, and bring it with you next week." So I did.

I ran into Pastor at our Wednesday night Bible study. He came up to me and asked, "You ever done any coon hunting, Dennis?" I replied, "No!" "We're gonna go!" he ordered. "I have the best coon hound in town."

And go we did. I found myself and Pastor running

6

through cornfields in the freezing cold, in the middle of the night, with a hound bellowing in the distance.

As the weeks went by, Pastor continued to challenge me. I was playing guitar for his Sunday-school class and started to minister to others the way he ministered to me. He had me over to his home, talked with me, and encouraged me. He never brought my past up again. Periodically, when he walked by me in church, he'd say, "Hi, Dennis! How's it going? Hear from the wife yet?" I would reply, "No, not yet." He never said anything after that. He would go on to something else. I believe it was his way of reminding me of the commitment I had made to God to be faithful.

A man who treated me so harshly in the beginning had become more than my counselor—he was my friend. A very dear friend. When we first met he showed me the Truth. Through his counsel and encouragement in the word and encouraging me to minister to others, he showed me the Way back. In his friendship and the examples of the way he lived, he showed me the Life. The Christian life.

John, chapter 14, verse 6, reads: "Jesus said 'I am the way, the truth, and the life. No one comes to the Father except through me.'" From our first meeting of devastation, to coon hunting, to discipleship, and his life being an example for his Lord, all the time he had been pointing me to my Lord and Savior, Jesus Christ.

Ever since our first one-on-one, Pastor has answered many questions by showing me, the Way, the Truth, and the Life.

I would like to answer Pastor's first question. Remember the one? He asked me, "If three treatment centers, numerous counselors, and preachers couldn't help you, what makes you think a simple country preacher like

7

myself can?" The answer is found in the way God used David, a simple shepherd boy, without all the fancy armor, to take down and kill a giant of a man. David, through the power of the Lord, did what a nation of combat champions couldn't do—he killed the giant. My past life—the guilt, the alcohol, the cocaine, the bitterness—had made me a giant in the ways of the world. The Bible tells us the old man has to die before the new one can live.

The grace of our Lord, working through Pastor, did what treatment centers, numerous counselors, and preachers couldn't do—killed the giant. God had provided Pastor with three smooth stones: the Way, the Truth, and the Life.

Thank you, Jesus, for *Pastor.*

Chapter 3
You Can Learn a Lot from a Raisin

Raisins are the wrinkled by-product of the best-quality grapes. When you see them advertised, the promoters stress that their raisins are seedless, have been seasoned by the sun, and have the freshest taste. Personally, I like raisins. They're compact in their little boxes, and that makes them an easy snack to fit into a lunch box, briefcase, or one's pocket. They don't seem to ever spoil, no matter what the environment is like.

* * *

One of the most disrespectful attitudes I carried inside me was toward elderly people. I verbally referred to them as *raisins*. That attitude didn't show when I was trying to sell them a car, motor home, or truck. That's because they had something of monetary value to offer. Inside me I considered them the all-used-up part of society. I felt they had nothing to offer me except memories of a grandfather who'd ridiculed and humiliated me when I was at the ages of six through nine. I look back at Grandpa now and see a man who died feeling rejected, alienated, and extremely lonely.

My grandpa had all the traits of an old man who wished he had treated his wife and family better. I remember going to his funeral as a little boy, wishing he had treated me better. There were fleeting moments when he would express a desire to be a real grandpa. I remember

9

him watching me race across the yard with a kite on a string and having no success getting it to soar into the air. My kite would start to take off as the wind caught it, but after two spinning loops it would come crashing to the ground. The words, "Hey, boy! You need a tail on that thing!" still ring in my mind. Grandpa called me over to his chair, talked with me, and sent me on a mission of mercy to obtain the necessary materials to make a tail for my kite. "Get me some string and a newspaper from the house," he ordered. I raced off in a skip-type run to seek out the string and newspaper that would make my new toy soar the way it was intended to. With his large hands, he rolled up pieces of newspaper about three inches across and bound them together with string. There must have been a dozen of them all linked together. Don't ask me how, but after examining my kite, he knew exactly how many of those little rolls of paper linked together it would take to make my kite fly. Somehow I think he had done that before. As I took off running, that four-cornered, oblong toy of mine reached heights that would have been impossible without his knowledge and experience.

I realize today that my grandpa wasn't a bad man. My grandpa lacked the same thing my kite did: a source of stability, a faith in Jesus Christ to let him soar the way he was intended to. I don't believe my grandpa was able to accept the grace that comes from knowing the Savior. I had heard the tragedies in his past discussed by my mom, aunts, and uncles. My grandpa sat with us in church many times. The church Mom took us to was a church that was very scriptural and taught strongly of the eternal life through faith in Jesus Christ. I recall a new suit we got Grandpa when he was age eighty to wear to his first church appearance in probably fifty years. There were few times that I saw Grandpa smile—once in church with us, and the other time was on that infamous day when my kite hit the sky. I hope, I just hope, that Grandpa and I can fly an eternal kite in heaven someday that won't need the stability of a tail anymore.

* * *

You're probably wondering what happened to the disrespect I had toward elderly people. It's kind of funny how the Lord places us in an environment where we have to deal with our sin, like it or not. Aside from the many tragedies that had taken place in my life, a lot of which were self-inflicted, I found myself at age thirty-seven on an isolated ranch in the middle of Michigan. I had no car to get around in and the nearest store was five or so miles away. Living behind me in a small trailer was the grandma of the people that had taken me in. They were on vacation during my first nine days there and it got awfully lonely sitting in the house all by myself. As I was struggling to keep my mind off the sin that had isolated me from my family, I felt the need to talk to someone. I was reading my Bible and praying but something was missing, something a lot of Christians take for granted—*fellowship!* I figured, what the heck, At least I wouldn't think I was going crazy by talking to myself. So I walked back to the little trailer and knocked on the door.

After living in the city for so long, I wasn't accustomed to people leaving their doors unlocked at night and yelling, "Come in!" As I walked through the door, there stood an eighty-three-year-old lady, propped up by her walker, grinning. "You must be Dennis!" she exclaimed. It was like she was expecting me. I replied with, "Hi!" There was a tape player going and the man on the tape was telling a story. She shut the tape player off and said, "My eyes are failing me, so this is how I read." We talked for a while and I got to hear about her entire family tree. As I was leaving I thought, *Maybe she is a Christian and would like to share with me a series of tapes I have by Chuck Swindoll about Solomon.* So I popped the question: "Are you saved?" "My heavens, yes!" she exclaimed. "Been so for forty or so years!"

The tradition started there. Each evening I would go over and we would listen to the Chuck Swindoll tapes. At the conclusion of the Solomon tapes, Chuck shared how Solomon died a regretful, devastated old man because of his disobedience. Although Solomon was esteemed as being the wisest man who ever lived, he lacked the consistency with God that brings forth the peace and divine love that a child of God experiences as life here on earth draws to an end.

When we had listened to all the tapes, I found myself reading to Grandma from God's word. I grew to love her like my own grandma. I called her Grandma, too. I took her out to dinner. We went to church together, and—well, she became my best of friends. I thoroughly enjoyed pushing her around in her wheelchair and helping her get around in her walker when we went out to dinner. We even joked about going dancing.

The wisdom and counsel she gave me about my problems far surpassed anything I had ever heard. Grandma shared with me her hurts she had had over the years and told me how the Lord had helped her grow through them. I remember her giving me some grandmotherly advice a few days before I left. It went something like this: "Keep it simple, Dennis! It's easier to keep track of that way!" The *it* she was referring to was life in general.

This raisin I call Grandma gave me a new perspective

on my grandpa, whom I had held bitterness toward for almost thirty years. She taught me how to see him through the eyes of Christ. Grandma also taught me how to view myself that way.

Like my grandpa giving my kite the stability it needed to soar the way it was intended to, Grandma, through the power of the Holy Spirit, gave me the stability in Jesus Christ that would allow me to soar for my Lord the way I was intended to.

* * *

Grandma was the wrinkled by-product of a lifelong commitment to Jesus Christ. She was of the highest quality of people. She had no seeds of hardness in her heart. Her words were of the freshest of taste because she had been seasoned by the Son of God.

Personally, I like raisins. They fit into an important part of my ministry. No matter what the environment, a raisin that belongs to Jesus will never spoil.

You can learn a lot from a raisin!

Chapter 4
A Garment of Grace

Wanting to do something special for someone is always a blessing to the giver. When I had a country-style dress hand made for my wife, complete with all the lace, ruffles, and fringes that women like, I had no idea that the seamstress God sent my way would comply with my requests far above what I had dreamed possible.

As I verbalized each detail to Miriam, she nodded, smiled, and showed me pictures of material and lace, and she even had a sample of material for me to touch. I was so excited. I couldn't wait to have it finished. Each hour seemed like a day as I anticipated the finished product. I thought to myself, *I hope she hasn't forgotten. I hope she isn't too busy with other, more pressing projects. I wonder if she understands or if I even told her my wife's birthday is only a few weeks away.*

Some discouragement started setting in. As thoughts settled in my mind, I resolved myself to the fact that I couldn't make the dress myself, and I would have to trust someone who could.

This dress occupied about all of my mind. Shortly after my first meeting with the seamstress—like, only a day or so—the phone rang. It was Miriam. She said, "I have your wife's dress ready." I said, *"Already?!"*

I made arrangements to pick it up real soon (like, yesterday!). I got to Miriam and her husband's house after work and bounded up to the door. I slowed down as she opened the door. I tried to act casual, like, *no big deal.* She took me through the kitchen, and hanging up on a hook, there it was. "Oh, dear, it's—it's—beautiful. I had no—well, I had—uh—" I was speechless. The dress, in fact, was perfect in every sense. It was like she could see inside my head. I had evidently presented my requests appropriately, for it was magnificent. "Wait 'til Linda sees it. Oh, and it's done in plenty of time for her birthday."

I took it to work and the girls in the office drooled over it. I showed it to as many people as I could. Even the guys were envious. They asked me where they could get one done just like it. I smiled and said, "You can't. *It's one of a kind.*"

That night I prayed and thanked God for Miriam and the dress she'd made. While praying I had some requests to bring before God, and they weren't as simple as making a dress. You see, I was mailing the dress to my wife instead of handing it to her. My inconsistent walk with my Lord had driven us apart. About 2,200 miles apart. More distant than the miles was her trust for me.

As I prayed and listened, the Lord started speaking to me. "Dennis," he said, "before you can have your family back, you need to be consistent with me and trust in me and in me alone. Your life is like the material used on the dress. I've forgiven you because of your faith in Jesus. But you need to be sewn together. You must be patient. Although you got impatient with the dress, you must not become impatient with me. This has been one of your weakest points. I have given you some material to touch; it's called the Bible. I have given you a Tailor called the Holy Spirit. He will sew and place each piece of your life exactly the way he wants it. He will give you fringes and ruffles that your wife will love, trust, and respect. I will not forget your request. You have told it to me every night. Someday I will call you and say, 'It's ready.' You will stand back and look at yourself and value your walk with me more greatly than you ever dreamed possible. You will stand tall with your Lord and be a *Garment of Grace.*"

Chapter 5

Benders and Stoopers: Verses on the Seeds of Abuse

Part 1. Seeds of Abuse

As a boy I had many seeds planted in my little mind—some good seeds, some bad seeds. I recall from my earliest childhood the bad seed of a dad who cheated on Mom and finally left us for someone else. I didn't know Jesus as my Savior, but I learned in Sunday school that God would answer my prayers if I prayed. So I asked him to bring my daddy home. I was too young at age six to understand his answer. Then the tragic news came: my daddy had been killed in a helicopter crash. I remember very clearly sitting on my bed with Mommy as she shared the news. I recall the bitterness and anger spilling from my mouth as I told God what I thought of his answer. The lack of *acceptance* had become the obstacle in my life. It would take years for me to understand, admit to, and finally do something about that.

If a child lives with deceit, that child learns deception. If a child lives with divorce, that child learns it as an alternative. If a child lives with drinking, that child learns to be a drunk. All three of these traits my kids, before they'd reached the age of eight, would see administered by either Mommy or Daddy.

Certain Christian psychologists talk about and express how resilient a child is. The word *resilience* is defined

17

like this: "the property of a material that enables it to regain its original shape after being bent, stretched, or compressed."

Two years after the tragedy of my dad's death, I would be molested at a Boy Scout camp by a man I loved and trusted. As a child I had my little mind and heart bent, stretched, and compressed about as far out of shape as the fuselage of a jet after a crash into the side of a mountain. I carried this guilt and humiliating secret inside me. It wouldn't be until some twenty-nine years later that the bad seeds that had grown into trees, whose roots were deep and branched out into every part of my life, would be exposed, uprooted, and left at the cross. I went from prison at age twenty-one to numerous counselors and chemical-dependency treatment centers, and the answers just weren't there.

I had given my life to Christ in prison at age twenty-one. I had hope and what I felt was an unshakable faith. Little did I know that the enemy thrived on filtering through the unknown trash of my past, then flaunted it inside me, kept me quiet with guilt, and expressed it to my loved ones as unmentionable sin.

My wife and I had instilled in the minds of our children the good seeds of telling Mommy and Daddy everything. Little did my wife know how driven I was, determined that *no one* would ever touch our children in a bad way.

Part 2. Benders and Stoopers

When I arrived in the village of Nashville, a small town in Michigan, little did I know that a church—a great church, a church of Grace—would be there. The miracle my family and loved ones had prayed for for years would happen in that village. I brought nothing to Nashville Baptist Church except a trashed-out life of inconsistency, including alcohol and drug abuse, dishonesty with myself and others, emotional abuse of a wife who loved me, and a lot of other characteristics that go with the above listed.

I never will forget the opening words of Pastor's message. In a loud voice he addressed his congregation with this statement: *"The law kills! Grace stoops or bends!"*

"If we are to be a great church," he stated, "we must learn to *bend* or *stoop*." I was thirsty. I was hungry for answers. Week by week he dwelled on the subject of bending and stooping. He had his congregation repeat, "Bend, stoop," over and over back to him. "We all have a right to our opinion," he stated, "but it is through bending and stooping the way Christ did that we can be a great church." People went out of their way to get to know me and to get me involved in service. They didn't care about my past or what dark secrets were buried inside me. They were too busy bending and stooping. They told me, "You don't have to prove yourself worthy, Christ did that for you at Calvary. All you have to do, Dennis, is trust and obey."

At the evening service I learned through a series of movies by Dr. James Dobson—*What Wives Wished Their Husbands Knew about Women*—just how much damage I had done to my wife. Silence about my childhood hadn't been golden. It had been destructive. After the five-week series by Dobson, out of the blue, Pastor devoted the whole evening service to *child abuse*. I had never told him about my tragedy at Boy Scout camp. I started realizing the trash I had brought, without even knowing it, into my marriage. The devastation turned into confession as I realized how far Christ had stooped to keep me for his own. Through a series of miracles, there I was in a small town

19

I'd never heard of, surrounded by people who didn't know me but loved me; and God was ending some thirty years of anger, regret, confusion, and feelings of inadequacy. In the Bible are mentioned men who entertained angels without knowing that was what their visitors were. You can tell by reading, I was no angel. But if an angel were to come to Nashville Baptist Church and investigate anonymously, he'd report back to our Lord that he'd witnessed the best bunch of benders and stoopers he had ever spied on.

Acceptance became the cure to heal—I had to *accept* that I wasn't responsible for the actions of the man at camp who had violated my trust. *Accept* that I wasn't to blame for my father's actions. And, greatest of all, *accept* God's plan for healing—realize that I didn't have to live in guilt for what I hadn't done. There is room at the cross for victims.

Part 3. The Lesson and the Experiment

It is imperative that victims get godly counsel. Ungodly counsel teaches that it's okay to be angry and stay angry. I have seen hate in victims' eyes over ungodly counsel or no counsel. A Christian needs to live in the solution, which is Christ and forgiveness, not the problem, which is their continuing to rehash and dwell on sin—anyone's sin. David, whom God regarded as being "a man after God's own heart," opens the Book of Psalms with this statement: *"Blessed is the man who walks not in the counsel of the ungodly."*

* * *

I prayed today with forgiveness for that man who molested me. I pray he knows Jesus and will spend eternity with him. *I have Peace.* I hated him for twenty-nine years. I have asked God to forgive me for my hate. *I have Peace.* I accept God's Grace. *I have Peace.*

* * *

As parents we have more than the responsibility of our walk with Christ. It's our instruction from God's word to bring our children up in the way of the Lord. Christian parents have a lot of excuses for not planting good seeds. If you know Christ, you know what the bad seeds are. Here is what the Bible says about one who plants bad seed in the heart and mind of a child. Mark, chapter 9, verse 42, reads like this: *"And if anyone causes one of these little ones to sin, it would be better for him to be thrown into the sea with a large millstone tied around his neck."*

Children learn from what we do, not what we say. If you would like to test your child to see how resilient he or she is, take drugs and be a drunk, abuse your spouse, say one thing and do another, don't pray together, don't go to church together, be too busy for your family, flirt with the office secretary, have an affair, divorce your spouse, and place your family in compromising situations.

It's devastating to see what one unconfessed sin can do in a family. It's even more devastating to watch the results of retaliation with either conditional forgiveness or no forgiveness when people close to us don't know about or understand the problem.

In conclusion Jesus Christ is the *only* property of mine that enabled me to regain my original shape after being bent, stretched, and compressed. I found resiliency in the Grace Christ gave me. He gave me the power of accep-

21

tance, forgiveness, and trust in him with the long-term plan for my life that leads to eternal glory.

P.S.: Funny thing about benders and stoopers—they're contagious. I think I'll design a T-shirt. It will read, *"Be a Bender and a Stooper: Jesus Is."*

Chapter 6

Room D-214 and My Roommate Jesus

Being in God's perfect will had never been one of my attributes. Somehow the drive to find comfort by living in nice homes and having good jobs and all the material fringes had for many years overshadowed God's purpose for me and his plan for my life. The goals I had set for my life and that of my family were based on nice things and an image for others to see. Somehow my relationship with my Lord had been overshadowed with materialism and people-pleasing.

It wasn't until I found myself homeless and penniless, my family gone, that the shield that had been over my eyes and heart for so long began gradually to be dismantled. Day by day I started getting my spiritual vision back. When the shield was completely removed I found myself staring face to face with my Lord Jesus.

Perhaps one of the most godly couples I have ever known, Chris and Teresa, had opened their home up to me. The only rules that had been laid down were no drinking and no drugs.

For the first week that I stayed with them in their late-1800s-built house, I set up living quarters in the family room. Chris had made some comments about moving me up to D-214. When I asked him, "What's that?" he said, "Never mind, we don't have it ready yet." I passed it off as some joke. My mind was on more important things, like feeling sorry for myself.

A few days passed. I walked into the house after cleaning horse stalls all day. Chris said, "Follow me." He walked over to a door that I thought was the door to a closet. When he opened the door I saw a narrow stairway. He motioned for me to follow him. As I started up the stairway, I noticed that a five-year-old would have had trouble getting his feet to fit on those stairs. I went up on the balls of my feet so as not to lose my footing.

Upon reaching the top of the stairs I realized that someone had forgotten to remodel the upstairs. There wasn't any heating system, only whatever heat would come up the stairwell from the downstairs if the door was open. Chris came up to a door, and on the door was a tag that read D-214. Now, I hadn't noticed that all my clothes and what little personal possessions God had left me with weren't in the family room anymore. I was about to find where they were.

As Chris opened the door to D-214 and we walked in, my mouth dropped. Chris, in a positive voice, said, "Here's your new room." An attempt to describe my living quarters? Well . . . it goes something like this. The floor had been painted green over the original hardwood about eighty to one hundred years before. The wallpaper had a pattern of blue and green roses. The windows were old counterweight style, with ropes that used to go into the walls to hold them open. There was an old-fashioned coil-spring bunk bed that took some getting used to, and an old desk and chair of about the same vintage. I think they were probably the ones that Noah had taken on the ark with him. Another sarcastic thought had taken refuge in my mind: at least there was a ladder to the top bunk in case I wanted to have a buddy sleep over.

I started noticing some other things that had been put in the room. Like my clothes. Chris and Teresa had hung my shirts and slacks up, folded my T-shirts and, well, actually the room was quite tidy.

As the weeks went by I grew to love my little room, with the squeaky spring bed and my ancient desk. It was by that old spring bed that I, on my knees, had some serious talks with God. It was at that ancient desk that I would cry as I wrote to my wife and kids a long ways off.

I shared that room with a very special friend of mine. He didn't care what D-214 looked like or even what I looked like. He was concerned with what my heart and the motives in that heart looked like. As the days went by I became quite honest with my friend. I started forgiving others as I learned to forgive myself. I started loving others as I learned to love myself. I started caring for others as I learned caring for myself—all because my roommate Jesus forgave, loved, and cared for me *first*.

I was finally able to view myself the way others do: by what I did, not by what I said. The most valuable things I possess today are eternal. They are older than that ancient coil-spring bed and desk. They began a long, long time ago, on a cross, and were passed on to me in room D-214 by my roommate Jesus.

Chapter 7
My Friend Gary

For thirty-seven years, as long as I've been alive, I have always valued friends. It wasn't until I looked up the word in my trusty NIV-study Bible concordance that I was able to find a biblical perspective on a friend or friends. There were only a handful of verses for the words *friend* and *friendship*. This was surprising to me. The love of my Savior Jesus is described as the most complete and divine love. It is that love that sent him to the cross where he took my place. It is only because of that love that Christians are able to have a truly complete and divine love for another person. We've experienced that love personally and are able to pass it on to others.

In 2 Samuel, chapter 1, verse 26, we read of David mourning his friend Jonathan's death. It reads like this: "I grieve for you, Jonathan my brother. You were very dear to me. Your love for me was wonderful, more wonderful than that of a woman."

If ever two men were close friends who shared their hurts, laughs, and their Savior Jesus it was Gary and I. The unbeliever may say that would have been impossible in the short time that we had to get to know each other. But we know different.

Like I myself, Gary had broken family relationships, an inconsistent walk with God, and a self-will that sometimes ran out of control.

When our Sunday-school teacher introduced us at a cafe after church on Sunday, neither one of us had any idea that the events that would soon take place would bring us both closer to our Lord, be so trying, and yet endow us with a gift of compassion that neither one of us had known before.

Gary was no sissy. He was tall and stocky. He was stubborn and blunt in his speech. I believe God wanted for years to use Gary and take his stubbornness and blunt way of expressing himself and mold them into tools for his Savior. His face and neck were scarred and most of his teeth were missing. He shared with me one night at a Sunday-school pizza party that years earlier his car had been hit by a train. Yes! That's right! I said that his car was hit by a train. Obviously Gary had been inside the car. He didn't offer any more information, and I wasn't about to ask. I just said, "Oh! Really?"

At that same pizza party, we went out to his car. I sat in the passenger's seat. *Bam!* I got hit right between the eyes with the words *Born Loser*. That was what was stenciled on the passenger side of his dashboard. I told you I was a lot like Gary. I started exercising my blunt speech. What I said went something like this: "What kind of testimony is that? God says we're victorious! I want that removed!" Gary finally got two words in edgewise. "Okay! Okay!" he said. I told Gary, "You only have to change one word! You've got the first part right. Substitute *loser* for the word *again*. Then it will read, *Born Again*."

A few weeks had passed and I was over at Jerry's and Judy's, my Sunday-school teacher and his wife's house, when about halfway through dinner the phone rang. It was Gary. He was complaining of chest pains and soreness in his left arm. Jerry, Judy, and I rushed over and took him into Lansing to the hospital. A series of tests revealed he had an aneurism the size of an orange on the main artery that supplied blood to his brain. It not only encompassed the artery, it had also ballooned inside the heart itself. The doctors at the hospital said they wouldn't touch it. There is only one place that does this type of surgery. It is in Houston, Texas.

I prayed and prayed and prayed. "Lord, I want to be with my friend when he faces this with you." The doctors said the surgery would have to be done immediately, and that Gary was a walking time bomb in the condition he was in.

The next day God answered my prayers. God had provided a team of surgeons at the Henry Ford Hospital in Detroit, only a few hours away.

Gary's dad had shared with us the story of the broken relationship he and his son had had for years. It seemed that neither one had been willing to reach out to the other. His dad told me of Gary's accident years earlier. Apparently a train slammed into the driver's door as Gary was attempting to make the crossing. The train dragged Gary's car with Gary in it for a full city block. Gary's dad explained to me what Gary couldn't or wouldn't just a few weeks earlier. The teeth Gary was missing had been embedded in the window frame of the driver's door. He had had a broken hip. Both jawbones had been broken, and his head had swollen to almost twice its normal size. His spleen had had to be removed and his chest cavity had been crushed.

It was the chest injuries in this 1977 accident that had damaged Gary's aorta, the trunk the arteries branch from. For fourteen years Gary had been a walking time bomb, and up until a few days earlier only the Lord had known of it. Each day of life for Gary had been a miracle. Each day of life for any of us is a miracle, a gift, not to be taken for granted. But Gary's life, more than the lives of most, had been on the very edge, the same way his walk with his Lord had been for so long.

As I sat with Gary and his family, including two brothers, a sister, and his mother and dad, the minutes ticked down. We all prayed together while waiting for the surgeons to come and wheel Gary away. His sister and brothers were meek yet confident. Gary's mom showed compassion in her eyes and a certain helplessness—the kind of helplessness you see in a mother's eyes when her son's life is on the line. I recognized that look all too well. I have seen it in my mother's eyes and my wife's eyes. I looked at Gary's dad and saw a broken man. I felt that if ever a man wanted to turn back the hands of time it was Gary's dad at that moment. He had spoken of his regrets and now they were expressed in his eyes.

As they were wheeling Gary out of his room he looked up at me, with a peace about him, and said, "I'm worried about Mom and Dad." This type of compassion I had not seen in Gary. Suddenly my thoughts went to Calvary, where our Lord, not concerning himself with his well-being, hung humiliated on a cross for me. In what could be the last time I saw Gary until Glory, he demonstrated a type of godly character that astounded me.

I looked over at Jerry and Judy as Gary's gurney disappeared through the large double doors. I started crying. An overwhelming feeling came over me—a feeling that I needed to pray, right then! right there! Jerry placed his hand on my shoulder and said, "He's in the Lord's hands, Dennis." That was the most profound thing said that day. Gary had been in the Lord's hands for years. If ever anyone knew about placing one of God's children in the Lord's hands it would be Jerry and Judy. Five years earlier they had lost their twenty-one-year-old daughter to a brain aneurism.

29

I simplified things in my mind. Would my friend live or die? The waiting went on, minute by minute, hour by hour. They took Gary around noon and at 7:00 P.M. we still hadn't heard anything. I certainly wasn't about to encourage the surgeons to hurry up.

Finally one of his brothers stood up. There was Gary. Sure enough, on a gurney, going by the intensive care lounge, wheeled my friend. My first thought was, *He's alive!* The question of whether he'd live or die seemed to have been answered. However, when the chief surgeon came in and began to talk to the family my heart sank. "It was a lot worse than we saw on the test," he reported. The aneurism had affected all three arteries. "In order to make the necessary repairs," he said, "we had to shut down the blood flow to the brain." There was a question in the doctor's mind if Gary would wake up at all. And if he did, how much brain damage, the doctor asked, might he have due to the lack of oxygen to the brain over the prolonged period of time during the repairs to his heart and arteries?

My friend Gary, I thought. *Oh Lord, you have brought him this far . . .* I couldn't express the anguish that penetrated every part of me. I was there to be a support to Gary and his family. Now *I* was falling apart. God's grace through the Holy Spirit started speaking to me. "Peace," it said. "Be still," I heard. "Trust me," the voice said; "I am in control. This family needs to see my strength in you." I started getting my spiritual second wind. I thought about that stenciled insult on Gary's dashboard—Born Loser. I resolved in my mind that I would make sure that it would read Born Again no matter what the outcome was there in the hospital.

That night Gary's family, all but his mom and dad, went home. I stayed the night with them. The only thing that could have removed me would have been if the Lord himself had decided to Rapture me.

We went to our rooms and I prayed. The next sound I heard was a horn outside in the parking garage. It was morning. I flew out of bed, showered, and got dressed. There was a knock on the door of my room. It was Gary's dad. He yelled through the door, "I'll meet you in the restaurant." I finished getting dressed and raced downstairs. I walked up to the table. I saw expressions of relief. I could tell things were looking up. Gary's dad told me that Gary had woken up that morning—and he was talking. "Praise God!" was my response. I said very little about Gary over breakfast. I did, however, share with them about God's mercy. I told Gary's dad that it looked like God was giving him another chance to be a dad.

His eyes clouded up while his wife sat there grinning slightly. We finished breakfast and went up to Gary's room. I walked through the security door and went around the corner, and there was my friend Gary. He had tube after tube going in and coming out of him. He was real pale and he had an oxygen mask on that made him look like Roger Ramjet. His eyes were barely open, but he saw me and the corner of his mouth went up as if he wanted to grin. I leaned over, and in a distant whisper he asked me, "How's it going?" I thought to myself, *Here he is, tubed, catheterized, cut, stitched, taped, and masked, and he's asking me, "How's it going?"* I replied, "Great! And you?" The corner of his mouth went up again and he asked, "How's Mom and Dad?" I told him they were doing fine. Our visit was brief, as he started to doze off. Gary's dad went up to the bedside and I heard Gary say, "I love you, Dad." Gary's dad turned to me with tears in his eyes. As we exited the ward his dad exclaimed, "That's the first time I can remember him saying, 'I love you.' "

Gary's parents left later that day and I decided to stay one more day. Visiting hours ended at 8:00 P.M. I sneaked up at 11:30 P.M. that night, and Gary's nurse let me in to visit. I had my Bible with me, so we had our devotions together. I read to Gary from Colossians, chapter 2, verses 6 and 7. It reads like this: "So then, just as you received Christ Jesus as Lord, continue to live in him, rooted and built up in him, strengthened in the faith as you were taught, and overflowing with thankfulness."

A thought came to my mind. I hadn't seen Gary move his legs at all. I looked around. His nurse had stepped away. I whispered in his ear, "Gary, wiggle your toes." I focused in on the foot of bed. Sure enough, ten little piggies were moving to and fro. I whispered again in his ear, "Gary, move your fingers." Yep! He should have been a piano player with that type of action. I was about as overflowed with thankfulness as one of God's children could get.

As I lay in bed that night I thanked God for the skill of the surgeons who, by His grace, used their hands to repair Gary's heart. I started thinking about the repairs the Holy Spirit had made on spiritual hearts. I was there and blessed to watch God's mighty hands work in so many different ways in the life of Gary and his family.

I started thinking about my family and other families—husbands, wives, mothers, fathers, sisters, brothers, daughters, sons, mothers, and fathers-in-law, sons and daughters-in-law, grandmas and grandpas, whose lives could be so hurt because of one un-Christlike heart. Families are gifts. Each one of us should go out of our way to see to it that our love for one another is not damaged by bitterness or anger. We need only to forgive, no matter what the other may say or do.

The most important lesson that I learned in all of this is, the only sick heart is the one that can't forgive the way

Christ does—*unconditionally*! In Matthew, chapter 5, verse 16, Jesus said, "Let your light shine before men, that they may see your good deeds and praise your father in heaven." If our light is supposed to shine before men, how much more important is it that the light shine for our families to see? My encouragement is found in Ephesians, chapter 4, verses 29 through 32. "Do not let any unwholesome talk come out of your mouths, but only what is helpful for building others up according to their need, that it may benefit those who listen. And do not grieve the Holy Spirit of God, with whom you were sealed for the day of redemption. Get rid of all bitterness, rage and anger, brawling and slander, along with every form of malice. Be kind and compassionate to one another, forgiving each other, just as in Christ God forgave you."

If we harbor bitterness and anger, or take part in anything that hurts our loved ones, we mock the grace that Jesus provided for us at Calvary. Believe me, I've been there; and if you don't believe me, just ask *my friend Gary*!

Chapter 8
The Eternal Duck

Every person who trusts in Jesus should have the freedom in their life to escape life's trials and seek God's direction through his word, the Bible. It was one such day for me—a day of trials. Work and family problems were bombarding my mind, and I felt that inner peace with God threatened. I was working at a new job in a strange town and separated from my wife and kids by 2,200 miles.

I took my lunch break from work and found the oasis God had provided for that day. I sat on a grassy lawn by a large duck pond. It was peaceful and elegant in God's setting. Our pastor had used an illustration with geese in Sunday's sermon. It stuck with me, so I asked God to show me something from his word about these unique aquatic critters called ducks. I watched them for some time. There was nothing real special about them. All they were doing was swimming, quacking, and eating. I focused in on their eating habits, and guess what? Not all ducks eat the same way. As I observed these billed, feathered quackers eat, I was able to place them into three distinct eating categories.

Category 1. The Surface Feeder

This duck eats only what is on the surface of the water. It does this with little effort. This duck seems to eat just enough to sustain his life. On closer observation I found this type of duck does more quacking than all the others. He has a lot of time for quacking because most of his energy is spent on quacking rather than eating. He also appears malnourished.

Category 2. The Aggressive Diver

This is superduck. He eats well. Every plunge is underwater. He gets large amounts of food. He is healthy and doesn't do much quacking, except to tell others where the food is. Although a duck swims well on top of the water, ducks are not really built for scuba diving. However, God made them so they could play "sea hunt" with an eagerness to be fed.

* * *

As I watched these web-footed critters eat I thought about God's word. One can read one's Bible a lot like the way a duck feeds, and the results are quite similar.

The correlation between the "surface feeder" and a certain way of reading God's word is this: "I read out of obligation. I pay little or no attention to its intended results. Ah, but just give me some talking room and I'll have all the answers for you, me, and whatever business isn't mine. Some say I'm a meddler and a gossip. I'm a real quacker. To get me back in the 'aggressive diver' mode, I usually need someone of real godly character to confront me, rebuke me, and shove my beak back in God's word, thus giving me the right perspective and a real chance to look at myself. The godly man or woman who loves his or her brother or sister in the Lord has a biblical responsibility to do this out of love."

35

He or she who plunges into God's word, grasping all and every lesson pertinent to life, is known as the aggressive diver. He or she bears the real fruit of Christianity. That person is a praise to their Lord. No matter what crisis arises in life, he or she gives new meaning to the message found in Psalm 46, verse 10a—*"Be still and know that I am God."* Aggressive divers have the respect of employers, friends, and family, and there are examples of *peace* to be found in their walk with Jesus. Their eyes are fixed on eternity, and they patiently await that magnificent gift of Eternal Life with their Savior.

What about the *third* category? What about the duck who plunges deep and then doesn't eat at all? This duck isn't so cute. He or she is an abomination to the cross and an abomination in testimony before others. Not only are such people inconsistent in their walk, they also have long periods of carnality—to put it mildly. Their actions place doubt in the minds of the unbeliever—doubt about whether a Savior does or could exist. Their life is an obstacle in the road of salvation. Their families suffer a lot of disappointment as they watch the examples of sin. The enemy thrives on this one's actions as others watch. He or she justifies his or her actions with lies and deceit. It almost always takes a tragedy to wake this person up. When the shock hits, he or she is standing with all bridges burned and the desire for life just about gone. Some never do find their way back, and the Lord takes them home.

How devastating it would be to stand before our Lord with unconfessed sin. As we reviewed our life on Judgement Day we would see as Jesus looked on, just shaking his head in disappointment at a trashed-out life full of the wreckage of willful disobedience and rejection to the Savior who suffered so willingly because of his love for us. What would God the Father do? The answer is found in

Revelation, chapter 3, verses 15 and 16. It says, "I know your deeds, that you are neither cold nor hot. I wish you were either one or the other. So because you are lukewarm—neither hot nor cold—I am about to spit you out of my mouth."

Some may say, "Dennis, that was written to a church, not individuals." Let me share this. What do you get when you mix hot and cold? *Lukewarm*. Lukewarm Christians make up lukewarm churches. Oh, by the way, the proper interpretation for the word "spit" found in verse 15 of chapter 3 (Revelation) is *vomit*.

In Hebrews, chapter 10, verses 28 through 31, is another illustration of God's view of a category 3 duck. It reads like this: "Anyone who rejected the Law of Moses died without mercy on the testimony of two or three witnesses. How much more severely do you think a man deserves to be punished who has trampled the Son of God under foot, who has treated as an unholy thing the blood of the covenant that sanctified him, and who has insulted the Spirit of Grace? For we know him who said, 'It is mine to avenge; I will repay,' and again, the Lord will judge his people. It is a dreadful thing to fall into the hands of the living God."

So as not to place myself in the judgement seat of others, I would like to share a secret with you. I lived as a category 3 duck for years. I am an expert on his behavior and the results of his sin. It is by the Grace of God, and only that Grace, that I am here to share *the eternal duck* with you. There is hope and encouragement for the category 3 duck to be an *aggressive diver*. It's a tough pond to swim in for a while, but God's mercy and grace can overcome any obstacle. If this duck can be persistent and truly seek God's will through God's word, with prayer, fellowship, and godly counsel, he or she can be one of the *aggressive divers*. It's a slow process for this duck to learn new eating habits. Trust and credibility take time. Consistency in Christ and dedication to that consistency are the wings that allow this duck to fly again. Reaching out to others—you know, sharing with them where the food can be found—is the best way for this duck to persevere through the rough waters ahead. Here are some encouragements that I found in God's word.

Be an aggressive diver. Read God's word faithfully. Feed on it! Digest it! Live it! Husbands, love your wives as Christ loved the Church and sacrificed himself for her. Bring your children up in the way of the Lord. Share Jesus with the unsaved, for the time is near. Forget what is behind you and press on to the goal. Live a life worthy of the gospel; and when you stand before God he will say, "Well done, my good and faithful servant." Be the duck Jesus had in mind when you gave your life to him.

Be joyful, peaceful, loving, patient, kind, full of faithfulness, gentleness, and self-control: an *eternal duck*.

Chapter 9
Evidence of the Divine Healing

Healing often baffled me. I had seen divine healing in other marriages and in personal problems, such as alcohol and drug abuse. I have chosen these topics because they have devastated my life with tragedy. I have had several nonbelievers shower me with such questions as, "How did you stand up under such circumstances? It would kill me!" And on the other side, the so-called Christians would encourage me with the statement, "You have pulled this before. We don't want to hear the crying, we want to see the baby." I had worked hard for years, trying to win the approval of Christians and failing every time.

I would continue to return to my old ways, angry and hurt. I attended two different churches, 2,200 miles apart, with the same denominational name. One taught I had to prove myself worthy, and the other—well, the other taught me that I would never be worthy; that my worthiness is found only through what Christ did through his death on the cross. So I focused in on the exhortations of the non-believers, and guess what? People started getting saved. All around me people were coming back to the Lord or giving their lives to him. My joy was being manifested in unrighteous people, while the righteous—well, they're still trying to see the baby.

I feel blessed. I relate to these unrighteous people. God's plan for me was that I should do what Christ did. Minister to the unrighteous, not try to prove myself worthy to the righteous.

I was close to a situation in which a youth pastor with only a high-school education counseled a married woman with two small children that she might need to divorce her husband to get him to come around. The husband pleaded with the youth pastor that the adultery that was the grounds for his statement had taken place almost two years earlier and had been confessed voluntarily almost one year earlier. The wife had chosen at that time to forgive. The husband made this clear to the youth pastor, whose comment was, "It doesn't matter. She still has biblical grounds if you have ever shown infidelity."

Six weeks after the divorce was filed that same youth pastor counseled the husband to get a lawyer because the wife was making the most of the legal system. I was told this counsel had been administered over the phone to the husband in an abrasive, extremely loud voice. I struggled with this type of action from a man within the church in a leadership role. I went to the word to get my answers. In James, chapter 3, verses 17 and 18, I found my answer. It reads like this: "But the wisdom that comes from heaven is first of all pure; then peace-loving, considerate, submissive, full of mercy and good fruit, impartial and sincere. Peacemakers who sow in peace raise a harvest of righteousness."

The really sad part in all of this is, the youth pastor was the husband's brother. I have chosen this as an illustration, not only because I know of the situation well, but also to let the readers know that if this family is ever together again, it will be because of *divine healing*—healing done in spite of human involvement.

In John, chapter 5, is the story of what I believe is the most unique and divine healing Christ ever did. It was unique in that, first, Christ asks the invalid described in verse 6, "Do you want to get well?" Secondly, in verse 7, the invalid replies with this, "Sir, I have no one to help me into the pool when the water is stirred. While I'm trying to get in, someone else goes down ahead of me." This man looked to something other than Christ for healing. His focus was on the pool, not Jesus.

The invalid went one step farther to make an excuse for his inability to get well. His excuse appears in the words, "While I'm trying to get in someone else goes down ahead of me." The invalid didn't know who Jesus was, therefore he couldn't have had much faith, if any at all. In verses 8 and 9 of John, chapter 5, the divine healing takes place—a miracle by Jesus himself. It reads like this: "Then Jesus said to him, Get up! Pick up your mat and walk. At once this man was cured. He picked up his mat and walked." Here is a guy who didn't know Jesus, had little or no faith, made excuses for his condition, and had to be asked if he wanted to get well. This is divine healing at its best, administered by the Master Healer, the Lord himself.

So often those afflicted with physical, emotional, or even spiritual ailments would rather be on the so-called pity potty, looking for attention, sympathy, or approval from others for their methods rather than seeking divine healing from our Lord. The world can offer many alternatives outside God's boundaries, like divorce, ungodly counsel, and the so-called rights to stay angry and to take advantage of people, or to be right.

Our Lord can overcome any of the above obstacles. Our Lord can heal someone in spite of that person's staring at the Master Healer and not asking for help, or trying to mix a little worldly help in with the Master's help. The only problem with the above listed is, sin has its results. While receiving healing for past problems we create new ones that may and probably will take their toll down the road.

I would like to close with this: The husband in the illustration used earlier never got an attorney. Under the direction of godly counsel he refused to do any more indulging with the world. His counselor shared James, chapter 4, verse 4, with him. It reads like this: "You adulterous people, don't you know that friendship with the world is hatred towards God?"

I had the privilege of spending Christmas Eve with the husband. That was the day his divorce was final. As a result of his indulging with the world but finally taking a stand for his Lord, he lost all rights to his children.

I shared with the husband a story in Judges, chapter 15, about a man whom God had given a powerful gift, the gift of physical strength. The man's name was Samson. Samson had been instructed by God not to give up the secret of his strength. Samson was deceived and disobeyed God. Samson found himself the object of public ridicule. Everything that God had blessed him with was taken away. His eyes were plucked out by the enemy. He found himself blind and walking in circles to grind grain. As his hair began to grow back, so did his faith in God. Samson was able to regain his strength even though his eyes had been taken. He prayed this prayer, found in Judges, chapter 16, verse 28: "O Sovereign Lord, remember me. O God, please strengthen me just once more and let me with one blow get revenge on the Philistines for my two eyes."

I told the husband he had one more chance to take the enemy out. I told him Samson's hair began to grow when he decided to follow God's instructions and not fight by human wisdom. I said that although his family was gone he had one more fight left in him. I told him God's Grace would be strong as he shared his life and testimony before others. I told him to be prepared, that through his Lord he could destroy the enemy in people—the enemy that had kept him in bondage for so long. He should be prepared, I told him, to bring the temple down.

I was happy with the husband as he knelt by his Christmas tree and quoted Scripture—2 Corinthians, chapter 10, verses 3 to 5: "For though we live in the world we do not wage war as the world does. The weapons we fight with are not weapons of the world. On the contrary, they have divine power to demolish strongholds. We demolish arguments and every pretension that sets itself up against the knowledge of God, and we take captive every thought to make it obedient to Christ."

* * *

Do you want to get well? Yes? Then focus your eyes on the Master Healer, and "pick up your mat and walk."

Chapter 10
I Stand Amazed

Have you ever had instilled in your mind the need to visit someone you have never met? Preachers do it on a regular basis. Someone in the congregation, or perhaps an anonymous source, will leave a message on one of those little cards in the pew racks, saying that someone is in need. I used to doodle on those little cards. It would take my mind off the more important things, like, how the preacher's message could be applied in my life.

In my own words I wish to share a story Ann Landers wrote in one of her news columns:

I recall hearing about a pastor who received a card, via the offering plate, that was unique, and the situation it brought about was extremely funny. On the card was written this:

I know a lady whose name is Doris. She has sat by me in this church for years. I haven't seen her for weeks. I'm worried about her. She is very quiet and it doesn't seem like she likes to talk to people. Her address is . . .
—Anonymous

The pastor had been at this church for years, but he couldn't place the person or the name. His curiosity built up so much that he didn't bother to wait until visiting day. He drove to the address listed on the pew card and found himself in front of a neat little cottage-style house. The entire front yard was one giant floral arrangement. The walkway to the front door was a rose arbor about twenty-five feet long. As he approached the front door he admired the beauty. The sun fell in spots through the shade of the flowers and stems that surrounded him. Through an open window by the door he could hear a TV inside. He had noticed a car in the driveway, so he prepared his heart to meet this stranger who had attended his church for years and whom he had never met.

He knocked on the door and waited a few minutes. No answer. So he knocked again, harder. Still no answer. He yelled through the window by the door, "Is anyone home? It's your pastor!" Still no response. Feeling somewhat dejected, he took out one of his cards with the church name and his title on it and wrote this on the back and left it sticking in the door.

Revelation, chapter 3, verse 20: "Behold, I stand at the door and knock. If anyone hears me and opens the door I will come in and fellowship with her and she with me."

Grinning at his humor and feeling accomplishment in his attempt to reach out to someone in need, he knew in his heart that this message would reach Doris—and reach her it did.

The following Sunday after church the preacher was greeting people as they were leaving the morning worship service. Among all the compliments, smiles, encouragements, and handshakes, a middle-aged woman walked up to the pastor and handed him one of his pew cards, turned around, and walked away. He finished his farewells and looked at the card. On it was a verse from Scripture, and it was signed "Doris."

The words were from Genesis, chapter 3, verse 10, which says:

> I heard you in the garden, and I was afraid because I was naked; so I hid.

I heard this funny little story relayed to a congregation by a young man in his farewell speech to his home church; he was headed off to Bible college to enter the ministry.

Being a collector of jokes and funny situations, I thought about the message that followed this young man's introduction. At age eighteen this young man was answering his Lord's calling to the ministry. The young man shared how God's grace had helped him overcome the anger and bitterness he had wrestled with in his high-school years. I sat there amazed at his honesty and dedication to persevere for his Lord.

I was a few months shy of thirty-eight. It had taken me all of sixteen years after I was saved at age twenty-one to say, "Yes, I'll do it, Lord." I won't go into the carnality or the specifics of the self-will that had just about destroyed me spiritually, physically, and emotionally. If my parents had named me Israel it would have been appropriate. I was a chosen man of God who spent sixteen years as a spiritual yo-yo; up and then down, obedient and then disobedient to my Lord, who had given me gifts that I would use to shame him rather than glorify him.

Perseverance for his name's sake, and following through with what Christ's original plan for my life was, would take all of sixteen years after my discharge from the state penitentiary in Chino, California. When I was discharged from Chino at the age of twenty-one I was saved but stubborn. I recall my mom smiling at me and saying, "The Lord's got big plans for you, Dennis," to which I replied harshly, "I'm not going to be a minister." She looked at me, hurt, and stated, "I never said that you should be a minister. What gave you that idea?" I realize today I wasn't saying *no* to my mother, I was saying *no* to my Lord. Deep inside me I knew what God wanted. I had committed my life to him in prison. He graciously, through a series of miracles, got me out of prison in one year, instead of leaving me there to serve out my ten-years-to-life sentence.

I chose to hang on to the bitterness, anger, and regret of my humiliating past. Instead of accepting God's grace, I tried to cover up my guilt with just about everything carnality could offer.

Several Christians, none of whom had known my mother or the words that had passed between us some sixteen years earlier, encouraged me to seek God's will, as an evangelist or in the ministry. I think if there is such a thing as loving sarcasm from God, he would probably say this today: "You know, Dennis, it's not like I was asking you to go to Nineveh."

I knew very well the story of Jonah. I remember how I as a boy cut out the whale in my Sunday-school workbook and pasted it on paper. I also recall the little man who went with that large fish; I pasted him next to it. I did not know as a little boy that someday I would become that little man. I wish today that I could have spent only three days in the belly of a great fish. I'm sure my loved ones, who suffered from my disobedience to God, wish the same.

If you want to hear a cry for mercy from a man who went the other way, you should have heard me on the night that my divorce was final.

A similar prayer can be heard in Jonah, chapter 2, verses 2-9. It reads like this:

In my distress I called to the Lord
    and he answered me.
From the depths of the grave I called
    for help, and you listened to my cry.
You hurled me into the deep,
    into the very heart of the seas,
    and the currents swirled about me;
all your waves and breakers
    swept over me.
I said, I have been banished
    from your sight;
yet I will look again
    toward your holy temple.
The engulfing waters threatened me,
    the deep surrounding me;
seaweed was wrapped around my
    head.
To the roots of the mountains I sank
    down;
the earth beneath barred me in
    forever.
But you brought my life up from the
    pit, O Lord my God,
When my life was ebbing away,
    I remembered you, Lord,
and my prayer rose to you,
    to your holy temple.
Those who cling to worthless idols
    forfeit the grace that could be theirs.
But I, with a song of thanksgiving,
    will sacrifice to you.
What I have vowed I will make good.
    Salvation comes from the Lord.

"Those who cling to worthless idols forfeit the grace that could be theirs." This statement that Jonah made toward the end of his prayer leads me to believe that he not only ran away from God's calling but also replaced obedience to God's will with some worldly things to fill the void.

At the end of his prayer he makes the promise to God, "What I have vowed I will make good." What he's saying here is, "Okay, Lord, I've had enough. I will follow through with your plans, not heed my fears caused by my lack of self-confidence."

When you vow to God to be obedient and do what he asks, you'd best do it. If you do, the blessings are rich and exciting. If you choose to walk away and do your own thing, I can promise you a hell on earth.

I entered seminary last week—sixteen years after I was told to. God's mercy is great. His grace far surpassed my disobedience. And his love—well, *I stand amazed*.

Chapter 11
Above Ground Zero

There is something about being high up in a tree that gives a young boy or girl a feeling of exuberance. By the time I was ten years of age I had watched every Tarzan movie that had been made. Somehow being above everything and looking down on things that would normally hold the same altitude of ground zero gave me a sense of security. Sooner or later the authority figure in my life, that person known as Mom, would call me to dinner, and I was back to ground zero again. I left that false sense of security and the make-believe wild animals that became the illusion of dreams in my own "Wild Kingdom."

One of the most significant things Christ did before his death, burial, and Resurrection was deexalt a short, self-exalted tax collector from a sycamore tree. The small-in-stature Zacchaeus became a monument of what Christ can do in a man's miserable life. Shorty Zacchaeus was esteemed by the Romans as well as the Jews as being an extorter, a conniver, and a parasite of his own fellowman. I don't believe Zacchaeus was born a crook. I believe his self-esteem had been damaged because of his small build. I can just hear the cruelty of people's remarks—nicknames like Small Fry, Shorty, and Twerp were administered in his native language. Zacchaeus used the world's riches, a position of power, and worldly knowledge to cover up his feelings of inadequacy. It was curiosity that took him up the sycamore tree, where he felt exalted as he waited for a glimpse of the Savior. It was the command of Christ himself that brought Zacchaeus back to ground zero. As we see upon reading further in Scripture—and as, I'm sure, many of us have experienced or may still experience—Christ never brings us down to reality and just leaves us there. Not only did Christ forgive and save Zacchaeus, he also brought salvation to his entire house. We read in Luke, chapter 19, verse 8, that Zacchaeus wanted to do whatever it took to obtain forgiveness through faith in Jesus Christ. Zacchaeus, like many of us, had been brought down by Christ only to be exalted by Christ as a new man—through grace, that wonderful grace.

Feelings of inadequacy are the number-one emotional killers of both the Christian and the non-Christian. For the unsaved, feelings of inadequacy can be the tool the Holy Spirit uses to reach a man or woman and show them not only eternal security but also an inner peace here on earth, as was the case with Zacchaeus. For the Christian, feelings of inadequacy are the all-too-often used weapons of the enemy. Even loved ones feed the destructive fires of inadequacy with tolerated verbal cuts and disrespectful statements. I have personally been the recipient of such verbal hanging by religious leaders, relatives, and people I love. I have even been the recipient of this type of action and then, heard it claimed to be of God. After a good dose of religious law and verbal and emotional abuse from loved ones, I was ready for some Grace. The most powerful definition of the word *grace* I have ever heard is this: *the unmerited favor of the awesome, holy God, given freely, generously, and persistently.* Feelings of inadequacy are the prompters that keep the dishonest person lying, the thief stealing, the manipulator conniving, the drunk drinking, and the addict abusing. The bottom line for the Christian who partakes in any of the above listed is a distorted and broken relationship before God.

I can just imagine the words that passed between Christ and Zacchaeus as they walked from the sycamore tree to his house. The Standard of Righteousness was walking right beside Zacchaeus all the way home.

It was not long ago that Christ brought me down to ground zero, only to exalt me and remove my feelings of inadequacy. Nothing short of the Savior himself was able to reach me. I heard a seminary professor use a sermon illustration that described my feelings of inadequacy with my Lord and my wife. It seems that the professor and his wife had adopted a young woman who had been abused physically, spiritually, and emotionally. My feelings toward God, similar to those of this child, were this: when I did something wrong the questions within me before God were a soft, childlike voice from my heart; that voice asked my Lord: *Are you mad at me? Do you still love me? Do I have to go away?* I not only found myself asking my Lord these questions from the inside, I verbally asked my wife the same questions after ten years of marriage. My Lord answered, *I died for you! I forgave you! And I've got plans for you*. My wife—she divorced me.

A hymn that comes to my mind and has become one of my favorites is worded like this:

My hope is built on nothing less;
than Jesus' blood and righteousness;
I dare not trust the sweetest frame;
But wholly lean on Jesus' name;

On Christ the solid rock I stand;
All other ground is sinking sand;
All other ground is sinking sand. [†]

* * *

It was the authority of the word of God, the command of Christ himself, that brought Shorty Zacchaeus out of his miserable and spiritually nonfulfilling life-style. When Christ ordered him to ground zero, he responded. The result was eternal security for Zacchaeus and his family. Has the phony grandeur of your life-style covered up your feelings of inadequacy? If that plague is in your heart, ask Jesus to come into your life and you will be saved. If you're saved, feelings of inadequacy are the lies that keep you from a harmonious, spirit-filled, and abundant life with Christ. It's not who we are in people, it's who we are in Christ. If people are making excuses for you, they're feeding the fires of inadequacy. The terms the world gives to water down, dilute, and make excuses for sin are *dysfunctional* and *co-dependent*. The first man who ever lived was Adam. How did he learn to be dysfunctional or co-dependent? Remember Adam's reply to God after his sin. It's found in Genesis, chapter 3, verse 12. It reads like this: "The woman you put here with me, she gave me some fruit from the tree, and I ate it." This turkey blames his woman and even goes so far as to blame his Maker. The world can give sin any name it wants to. It's still sin and must be dealt with as sin—confessed, forgiven, and cleansed. After all, isn't that what it says in 1 John, chapter 1, verse 9? It reads like this: "If we confess our sin he is faithful and just

†Edward Mote and William B. Bradbury, "The Solid Rock."

to forgive us our sin and cleanse us from all unrighteousness."

When I was ready to admit to myself and my Lord that it was *my* fault and I had a choice to make, that I chose to do wrong, knowing what right is, I was able to accept forgiveness for myself, and then I could forgive others.

* * *

It was Christ who brought me out of my miserable and spiritually nonfulfilling life-style. I no longer have feelings of inadequacy, because Jesus adequately loves me, adequately forgives me, and adequately restored me to righteousness. When Christ ordered me to ground zero, I responded. I have been walking next to the Standard of Righteousness ever since; exalted by Christ and far above ground zero.

Chapter 12
Contaminated Food

There's a restaurant, a favorite of mine, that I used to stop off at on my way home from seminary. It's known for speedy service, good food, and being affordable. Everyone on the staff there appeared to be enjoying themselves as they greeted customers with smiles and an attitude of enthusiasm. As I got to know the manager, and after talking with him for some time, I found out it was all a facade. In fact the same night that I talked to the manager a middle-aged lady and her husband walked out. They were upset. I heard them voice their opinion of what they thought of the foreign material they had found in their food. When confronted, the waitress offered to give them the meal for free. That wasn't enough, they told her. The waitress's attitude then turned rough, malicious, and verbally abusive.

Anyone who knows me or has sat down with me for one meal is aware of the fact that I love to eat. To me, food is one of the seven wonders of the world. I am looked upon by many as being a *pig*. For me, nothing can ruin a good meal! Well . . . almost nothing. That night when Mrs. Whoever found whatever in her who knows what, I stopped eating. I started examining the contents of my plate to see if I had been served even a little portion of contaminated food. My food looked okay. But what if I had eaten something bad the last time I was in here? Maybe I hadn't had the flu a few weeks before. Maybe I ate some little critter that was a carrier of—of . . . I hailed the waitress. "May I have my check, please?" So much for my favorite restaurant.

On my way home I thought about a statement my seminary professor had made to a pastor he was counseling. He shared it in real general terms so as not to break the confidentiality of his counsel. The preacher had made the comment that he didn't care for Billy Graham. He stated, "He's too shallow!" Now the pastor was meeting with the professor regarding various problems within his church that overwhelmed him, one of which was the gradual decline of membership and attendance. The professor answered the comment with this: "Billy Graham," he retorted, "packs an entire football stadium night after night. Thousands upon thousands come to know Jesus as their personal Savior from Dr. Graham's life's testimony and his preaching. You're here, Preacher, struggling to keep a church roster of one hundred and seventy-five members. Did you ever stop to think that maybe *you're a little too deep!*" Amen, Doc!

I was in seminary to answer God's calling to reach sinners for Christ. The professor says we're seed sowers. To be too deep is to sow seeds with steel jackets on them. This brings to mind an old chorus sailors used to sing: "Many brave hearts are asleep in the deep; so beware!"

Jesus was too shallow for many. Let's take a look at how Isaiah, in his fifty-third chapter, describes the Savior. Pay close attention to verses 2 and 3. They read like this:

He grew up before him like a tender
   shoot, and like a root out of dry ground.
He had no beauty or majesty to attract
   us to him.
Nothing in his appearance that we
   should desire him.

He was despised and rejected by man.
  A man of sorrows and familiar
    with suffering.
Like one from whom men hide their
  faces.
He was despised, and we esteemed
  him not.

If you would like to hear about the shortest sowing and planting time, and the quickest salvation prayer ever spoken, take a look at the Savior as he hung on the cross. Remember the thief next to Christ as described in Luke, chapter 23, verses 41 through 43. The description reads: " 'We are punished justly, for we are getting what our deeds deserve. But this man has done nothing wrong.' Then he said, 'Jesus, remember me when you come into your kingdom.' Jesus answered him, 'I tell you the truth, today you will be with me in paradise.' "

I think about the example that hung before the criminal. It didn't take many words to bring this man to salvation. I think to myself, and I ask this question: *Is my life sacrifice the living example of sacrifice? Do I follow the example who hung on the cross? Or do I have to fill in the blanks with fancy words?*

I heard many fancy words from a preacher at the church I was a member of and had been a member of for five years. I am a seminary student now, and I realize today the negative impact this individual's actions had on me spiritually. The trials I experienced at the church I attended with my wife and two kids were more draining spiritually than the abuse of alcohol and drugs that I was trying to overcome. I watched member after member leave to join other churches. The most devastating thing that took place there was the excommunication of the associate

57

pastor. I will never forget the unbiblical stage show that the pastor put on in order to justify his actions against the associate pastor. The associate pastor was a dear friend who had spent many a night talking with me; we had done much sharing in our Lord. I attribute much of what I am today to the seeds he planted in my heart, the seeds that others watered and the Holy Spirit made grow. The word *methodology* was the fancy word that was the basis for the pastor's excommunication of the associate pastor. I couldn't find the word in Scripture. For a long time I didn't know what the word meant. I confronted the pastor on the issue in his office. In the course of our conversation he gave up two confidences I had no need to hear. They were not pertinent to the situation. Even if they had been, the information he shared, in the wrong hands, could have destroyed another family not involved with the situation. If you would like to hear something *deep*, the definition of the word *methodology* from *Webster's New World Dictionary* reads like this: "the branch of logic concerned with the application of the principles of reasoning to scientific and philosophic inquiry."

I realize today that God used this tragedy, just as he uses all tragedies. I remember today when I speak, write, counsel, and share discipleship with people what kind of impact the fancy words had on me. I look to the cross, and when I turn to my fellowman I see a simple sinner dying because he needs Christ. The words come from my heart, where my Jesus lives.

Words from a pastor, teacher, or counselor are food for the soul. If there is anything other than Christ in those words the food is contaminated. Contaminated food can be administered with a smile or an attitude of enthusiasm. How can one tell if food is contaminated? If the church is truly a *church of Grace*, there will be pardon and partying.

58

If the church has contaminated food, there will be fighting and feuding. If you confront the server of food and that person's attitude is rough, malicious, and/or verbally abusive, you need to find another waitress, or eat in a different restaurant.

Chapter 13
The Innocence of a Child

Being a father of two, a boy and a girl, I never ceased to be amazed at the things that would come out of a child's mouth from the bottom of its little heart. Sometimes it was funny or dumbfounding, and depending on the environment, the little words of innocents had proved to be extremely embarrassing at times.

This subject brings to mind a story I once heard of a little boy who was extremely disruptive in church. Week by week from the pulpit the pastor would watch Daddy exit with this little tyke. The rod of correction could be heard throughout the hallways and sanctuary.

The pastor approached Mom and Dad after church one Sunday. "Would you mind leaving your son with me for the afternoon?" he asked. They agreed to that. The pastor took the little boy by the hand and proceeded to give him a tour of the church. From the choir loft to the boiler room, the preacher showed the little boy the entire building. The little boy said nothing the whole time. As they were walking down the hallway to the exit, the little boy noticed a group of pictures of men in uniforms hanging on the wall. The little boy spoke his first words. "What's that?" he asked. The preacher answered, "This is a memorial of the men who were members of our church who lost their lives in the service." The little boy's eyes clouded up and his little lips started quivering. The little boy looked up at the preacher. As the tears started running down his cheeks

60

he asked, "Sir, was that at the morning service or the evening service?"

Throughout the Bible God tells us that we Christians must keep our hearts soft, like that of a child. So often our religion becomes complicated with its so-called dos and don'ts. We forget about the grace, that wonderful grace, that Christ paid such a high price for with his suffering and death at Calvary. In Mark, chapter 10, verses 14 and 15, Jesus said, "Let the little children come to me, and do not hinder them, for the kingdom of God belongs to such as these. I tell you the truth, anyone who will not receive the kingdom of God as a little child will never enter it."

The Bible tells us we must grow in our faith by reading God's word. Our trust is found in prayer and our fellowship equips us and gives us the opportunity to reach the unsaved. If reading God's word, prayer, fellowship, and ministering to others are not done with a childlike heart, we can expect little or no results in our spiritual growth and in our testimony before others. I believe our Lord Jesus would rather we embarrass him with simplicity than try to hammer into people doctrine that they just don't understand. Sound doctrine is important. It is the essence of what we believe. But doctrine should be administered with a childlike heart. We mustn't confuse head knowledge with heart knowledge.

Throughout the Bible, God asks men to return to him. Get back to the basics, would be a good interpretation. In Revelation, chapter 2 verses 4 and 5, Jesus warns the entire church of Ephesus. In the preceding verses Jesus praises them for their hard work and perseverance, for not tolerating wicked men, and for their endurance of hardship for his name's sake. But in verses 4 and 5 of chapter 2 of Revelation Jesus warns them. It reads like this: "Yet I hold this against you: You have forsaken your first love. Remember the height from which you have fallen! Repent and do the things you did first. If you do not repent, I will come to you and remove your lampstand from its place."

"Do the things you did first!" That's the key to the childlike heart. We must never lose sight of where we came from, and the wonderful grace that got us where we are today.

What's wrong if our innocence before God is pure, like that of a child? It had better be. Let my prayer continue to be that I maintain in my heart *the innocence of a child.*

Chapter 14
The Child I Never Knew

Our society teaches through television, radio, music, and ungodly counsel that a man needs to be the so-called macho man—the don't-cry-it's-a-sign-of-weakness type of man. There are even some churches that teach that the man is the spiritual backbone of the family. This lie and others are the reasons why the Christian family is threatened and the divorce rate has skyrocketed within the church.

The truth is that Jesus Christ should be the spiritual backbone of any Christian family. The husband and wife should complement each other through the power of the Holy Spirit. They should share mutual respect and love and compassion; they should be sensitive to each other's emotions. Tears must be shed together over tragedy and sorrow. Ephesians, chapter 5, verse 25, says, "Husbands, love your wives, just as Christ loved the church and gave himself up for her."

You ask the Christian husband, "Would you die for your wife?" You can rest assured that all would say, without a second thought, "Of course," or a definite "Yes!" That's the macho man speaking. Statistics that result from talking with wives show that the majority of men are lacking in or can't even share with their wives at least one of the following: mutual respect, love, hurt, emotions, and being able to cry with the wife over sorrow. If a husband can't cry with his wife, what makes him think that he could sacrifice his life to spare hers? There has been a lot said about the pro-life and the abortion issues, in the media as well as in the church.

A subject that has touched many Christian homes and has little written about it is the unwilled loss of a child—a child that God takes before birth, a miscarriage. I remember hearing a preacher speak on miscarriage a few years ago. Obviously he was a man. Certain words of his—"The child goes to be with the Lord"—stuck with me. He was so vague it makes me sick to think of it today. We as Christians know the child goes to be with the Lord! What about the family—the wife or the husband?

This is where we find out who the spiritual backbone of the family is. The preacher sends the fetus to heaven. The husband goes to work the next day; and the wife? The wife—she cries out from the deepest part of her heart at the loss of this little life that grew inside her.

There are many preachers who are fine family men and whose lives are examples of the godly husband. It is in them that wise counsel should be sought by both husband and wife in this time of sorrow. There isn't a job around worth the harmony that could be lost in the devastation a miscarriage can bring into the home. Children are gifts from God, they are his to give or not give. Dealing with the tragedy of miscarriage must be done in a Christlike manner. If the husband can't get away from work, he needs to find a job that will allow him the time to do what God says he must: *Be there!* Any job that doesn't allow for the value of human life isn't worth having.

If a husband could look inside his wife's heart the way Jesus does after their loss, he would find inscribed this poem:

I was so happy when the doctor confirmed my suspicions.
I thought about your little cuddly body pressed against

mine. I contemplated names as the questions would arise: Is it a boy, or is it a girl? Will it wear pink, or will it wear blue? I never dreamed you would be *The Child I Never Knew*.

I felt your little legs kick, I anticipated your every move, I anxiously awaited your arrival with a grin. I shared the news with friends as they shared in my joy. You must have been special for the Lord to want you so soon. You were taken from me by an angel. On wings to heaven you flew. Thank you, dear Jesus, for blessing me with *The Child I Never Knew*.

Chapter 15
Paid in Full

If you would like to hear a statement that is somewhat mind-boggling, lets your thoughts run in several healthy directions, and can be very convicting, try this on for size: "A person's repentance should be as notorious as their sin!" After repeating this to myself at least a dozen times, over and over, I came to the conclusion that this could be an understatement, and in most cases it has become a minimum requirement.

In 2 Samuel, chapter 12, from verse 1 through verse 4, Nathan gives King David a scenario. David listens to Nathan as the prophet of God describes a man's activities. King David burned with anger, as described in verse 5 of 2 Samuel, chapter 12. I'll quote David from Scripture. This is his assessment of what should happen to the man whose actions were described in this parable by Nathan: "As surely as the Lord lives, the man who did this deserves to die! He must pay for the lamb four times over, because he did such a thing and had no pity." David, esteemed by God as a man after God's own heart, says the man deserves to die, not that the man must die. If any child of God got what he or she deserved we would all be spending eternity in hell. I find it interesting that David used payment for the Lamb as the alternative to death. Down the line of his ancestors the Lamb of God, Jesus Christ, would become the Lamb to pay for all of mankind's unjust and sinful actions. I'll quote John the Baptist as he, in John, chapter

1, verse 29, introduces Jesus: "Behold the Lamb of God who takes away the sins of the world."

I'm sure God has burned with anger at me many times for my actions. I am eternally thankful God has provided a Lamb for full payment. For David, payment for the Lamb four times over was the law of that day. For Christians, the Lamb of God, which is Jesus, becomes the payment. It's not all that hard to understand. Under the law we have to pay for the Lamb. Under Grace the Lamb paid for us. I believe if David had condemned the man Nathan used in his illustration, he would have sealed his own fate. Obviously this was not in God's plan. It is through the lineage of David that our Lord Jesus would be born. I'm sure one could just imagine the expression on David's face and the shock in his heart as Nathan told David, in 2 Samuel, chapter 12, verses 7 through 10, "You are the man! This is what the Lord, the God of Israel, says: 'I anointed you king over Israel, and I delivered you from the hand of Saul. I gave your master's house to you, and your master's wives into your arms. I gave you the house of Israel and Judah. And if all this had been too little, I would have given you even more. Why did you despise the word of the Lord by doing what is evil in His eyes? You struck Uriah the Hittite with the sword and took his wife to be your own. You killed him with the sword of the Ammonites. Now, therefore, the sword will never depart from your house, because you despised me and took the wife of Uriah the Hittite to be your own.' "

David's plan was internal; however, the actions it brought forth were external. Adultery, murder, manipulation, conniving, deception, and betrayal of a friend became the external results of David's internal sin. Jeremiah the prophet couldn't have described it better when he quoted our Lord's words, found in Jeremiah, chapter 17, verses 9 and 10. It reads like this:

The heart is deceitful above all things
   and beyond cure.
   Who can understand it?
I the Lord search the heart
   and examine the mind,
to reward a man according to his
   conduct,
according to what his deeds
   deserve.

* * *

I made a commitment to God that I would never again ask Him to give me what I deserve. After placing requests before God to give me the job I deserve, the family I deserve, the house I deserve, and the money I deserve, I found myself unemployed, divorced, homeless, penniless, and literally shoveling animal waste for room and board. Today I thank him for the grace he has given me—*the unearned grace*.

So often our desires become obsessions. We do or say anything to get our own way or have what we want. We take our focus off pleasing God and think we can have it our way for a while. Like King David, we use the power at our disposal to try and find happiness or the old compromise of the end justifying the means. For the Christian, *the end never justifies the means*, as already described in Jeremiah 17, verses 9 and 10.

Have you asked God to give you what is rightfully

yours or what you deserve? I hope not! If you know the Savior and you make such a request you'll probably get what you ask for!

Chapter 16
The Division of a Child

"Daddy, I pray for you to come home, every morning on my way to school. When I ride the bus, I think about you, Daddy. I cry, Daddy! I miss you, Daddy!"

My seven-year-old son shared these words with me over the phone last Christmas Eve. I asked him, "Tim, did you know that Mommy is divorcing Daddy?" "Yes, Daddy!" he replied. "Mommy says it's part of God's plan." A shiver ran down my body and I straightened up and said, "Son, divorce is man's plan. God's plan for marriage is based on grace and forgiveness, and for better or for worse." I paused and thought to myself, *He's only seven and a half! What are you doing calling his mother a liar?* At that point I realized that I was going to have to give the rest of that ugly situation to God. I haven't talked to or seen my son or daughter since. I had chosen not to fight with an attorney in court. I was at the mercy of the divorce as my wife and her attorney had written it—or was I?

I found myself in seminary shortly after my divorce was final. I won't go into the series of miracles that put me there. However, I was learning God's word like never before. The seminary professors who were teaching and challenging me were aware of my situation. They knew of the counsel my wife and I had received throughout our ten years of marriage. They even knew some of the preachers and people who had counseled us. They were appalled, to say the least. The thoughts of blaming myself and others, including my wife, started to shift. I began to realize who had really been at work in my marriage. The crafty father of lies had manipulated the thoughts and actions of each person involved. Each of us responded just like little puppets to the prewritten script of divorce. The cast of characters can be described as follows: a husband with extreme feelings of inadequacy; a wife with low self-esteem; meddling in-laws on both sides; and a misinformed, uneducated youth pastor, who was also a relative, operating on secondhand information. Actually, you can watch this type of story line on the afternoon soap operas. The world finds it very entertaining and profitable.

Children find it hereditary. There are at least three generations of divorce on my wife's side of the family, and my side has had too many to count.

In each case, the kids lived in a split household and learned that daddies become visitors—weekend heros, so to speak. My children saw two different role models with two different opinions of how things should be done, should not be done, who's right, who's wrong; God says this, God says that; and someday, my son and daughter will be telling their little boy or girl, "It's all part of God's plan!"

I'll never forget one preacher's telling me that my wife was divorcing me because of my inconsistent walk with God. Another one told me that she would come back when I proved myself. I had already burned myself out trying to prove myself. Neither of these pastors had ever been to our house or talked to me about our marriage.

All my professors and instructors in seminary encouraged me not to listen to anyone but God. Oh, I have several I am accountable to for guidance on how I should spend my time in the word, for fellowship and spiritual growth, but they would not give me an absolute ruling on how to deal with the tragedy my children were feeling.

They would remind me about God's grace and encourage me to search his word and be sensitive to the Holy Spirit's leading. I prayed and prayed and asked God to show me the truth in his word. I asked the Lord to give me wisdom ... Wisdom? *Wisdom!*

I had been baffled for months concerning the course of action to take as far as my kids were concerned. Every part of me said *Get a lawyer! You pay support! You can tell them the truth!* My heart already ached from the loss of my wife. Every human, fatherly instinct told me to fight. I had fought for years and tried to find happiness and to get my wife to love me and forget the past. I would have agreed to or said anything to keep her.

God has shown me that only He is worthy of that type of love. My wife had become an idol. I couldn't let my kids take on that role. I didn't want my children to grow up thinking divorce was a way to get Daddy to behave the way Mommy wanted. They needed to trust in the Lord, not in another human's sin.

In 1 Kings, chapter 3, verses 16 through 28, there is an account of a godly decision, based on genuine parental love, in an ungodly situation. Read carefully the scenario and you'll see how God's wisdom through King Solomon prevailed over sin. "Now two prostitutes came to the king and stood before him. One of them said, 'My lord, this woman and I live in the same house. I had a baby while she was there with me. The third day after my child was born, this woman also had a baby. We were alone; there was no one in the house but the two of us. During the night this woman's son died because she lay on him. So she got up in the middle of the night and took my son from my side while I your servant was asleep. She put him by her breast and put her dead son by my heart. The next morning I got up to nurse my son—and he was dead! But when I looked at him closely in the morning light, I saw that it wasn't the son I had borne.' The other woman said, 'No! The living one is my son; the dead one is yours. But the first one insisted, 'No! The dead one is yours; the living one is mine.' And so they argued before the king. The king said, 'This one says, "My son is alive and your son is dead," while that one says, "No! Your son is dead and mine is alive." Then the king said, 'Bring me a sword.' So they brought a sword for the king. He then gave an order; 'Cut the living child in two and give half to one and half to the other.' The woman whose son was alive was filled with compassion for her son and said to the king, 'Please, my lord, give her the living baby! Don't kill him!' But the other said, 'Neither I nor you shall have him. Cut him in two!' Then the king gave his ruling: 'Give the living baby to the first woman. Do not kill him; she is the mother.' When all Israel heard the verdict the king had given, they held the king in awe, because they saw that he had wisdom from God to administer justice."

* * *

"Neither I nor you shall have him. Cut him in two!" These words bounced around in my head and finally drifted to my heart. Was I willing to divide my children? Is that the type of love a godly man has for his children? My heavenly Father gave his Son Jesus up for me; certainly I could go against the ridicule of people telling me I didn't love my kids and be willing to give them up completely for the cause of Christ. After all, they were the same people who operated on half-truths and followed the standard operating procedure of the world rather than the grace Christ had once showed them. I was tired of acting out the standard, predictable role according to worldly

73

wisdom. That in itself was one of the main reasons my family and I were apart. Someday my children would see a changed Daddy. They would know from my example and ministry that I serve my Lord first. Outside the standard operating procedures of the world, God has assured me from his word that someday my children will know that *divorce is never part of God's plan!*

A real daddy doesn't wish to have his children divided. He is willing to give them up in order to live in oneness.

> Do not conform any longer to the pattern of this world, but be transformed by the renewing of your mind. Then you will be able to test and approve what God's will is—his good, pleasing, and perfect will.
>
> —Romans 12:2

Chapter 17

"?"

He sat in our living room at about 9:00 P.M. on Sunday evening. He was my roommate's guest at our Bible study for singles. He reeked of booze and his speech was somewhat slurred. He was outspoken and had no qualms about sharing his personal life. I paid little attention to him—that is, up until he made this statement: "I'm an alcoholic and a homosexual, and I can't find a job!"

I don't believe anyone had ever introduced themselves to me like that before. I looked at him and thought to myself, *Now here's a real loser!* I had had my bouts with drinking and drugs and other worldly indulgences, but I in no way wanted anything to do with a queer. I was taking a class in seminary called Evangelism 104. I went to bed that night and this guy's statement rang in my mind over and over. I found myself a couple of hours later still thinking, dwelling on what had happened and wondering what in the world my roommate was doing letting this less than desirable element into our apartment. I mean, after all, Scripture is very clear on homosexuality.

The Holy Spirit has given me little room for a holier-than-thou attitude. Although I had never been a homosexual, you can tell by reading previous chapters that I had every reason to hate this guy—every reason except the grace that Christ had shown me not too long before. Since my commitment to the ministry, I get convicted very harshly inside when my heart starts to go out of bounds. I found my mind changing and dwelling on

Scripture. Therefore a passage in Isaiah, the 53rd chapter verse 6, that reads like this: "We all, like sheep, have gone astray, each of us has turned to his own way; and the Lord has laid on him the iniquity of us all." The words rang clear in my mind, and the little voice I once heard in a corral of soupy manure said, "Dennis! I died for this guy too. I'll judge him. You do your job and start planting seeds." I started praying for this guy and asking the Lord to direct my attitude and my words the next time we met. I said amen and went right to sleep.

I haven't mentioned this guy's name for a good reason. I had heard a joke. God used this joke and it became very significant in my future friendship and testimony to "?." I shared the joke with the guy in question. The joke goes something like this:

A little boy exited his Sunday-school class grinning from ear to ear. His mother questioned him: why did he have that beaming smile on his face and the lit-up expression in his eyes?

Mother: Well, tell me, what did you learn in Sunday school?
Little boy: I learned God's name today!
Mother: You did what?
Little boy: I learned God's name.
Mother: Well, tell me, son! Just what is God's name?
Little boy: Howard!
Mother: Howard? Where did you come up with that?
Little boy: You know, Mom! Our father who art in heaven, *Howard* be thy name!

You guessed it. The less-than-desirable element I have been referring to as *this guy* is named Howard. Most nicknames are short and improper. The joke made everyone laugh, and, well, Howard's name was extended; it became Howard Be Thy Name. That is about as proper as English can get. I'll never forget the expression on Howard Be Thy Name's face when I told him the punch line.

A different expression, one of deep conviction, came across Howard's face when I shared, not another joke, but one of my stories. I read the chapter of this book titled "Above Ground Zero." You have probably read the chapter, which is about feelings of inadequacy and how I had tried to cover them up. You can imagine the expression on Howard Be Thy Name's face when I shared the words, *"It was Christ who brought me out of my miserable and spiritually nonfulfilling life-style. I no longer have feelings of inadequacy, because Jesus adequately loves me, adequately forgives me, and adequately restored me to righteousness."*

Howard Be Thy Name has a degree in psychology and works as a mental health technician. As he started side-stepping and talking from his head knowledge, I prayed inside: *Lord, you've given me such a burden for this man. Please, in your name, Jesus, give me the wisdom to answer Howard.* I listened to the words of confusion and the circles Howard talked in. Then the Holy Spirit started speaking to my heart. "Sound familiar, Dennis? Aren't those the same words and thoughts that were used on you? Aren't they the same ones the secular world confused you with for almost thirty years? Remember the simplicity I showed you through a fifty-two-year-old country preacher and a raisin called Grandma."

I leaned forward and looked Howard right in the eyes and said this: "I'm not impressed with your wisdom. It did me no good and it's got you confused about the truth. If that head knowledge of yours did any good you wouldn't have been sitting here a few weeks ago complaining about being an unemployed homosexual drunk. The only problem you have, Howard, is sin. It's not unique. We all have it. That's why you need Jesus Christ as your Lord and Savior. You see, Howard, when Christ went to the cross, he paid for all that trash you have been packing around. It's a simple plan. When Jesus said, 'It's finished!' that's what he meant. There is nothing else that needs to be done. The plan is complete with Christ. Man has distorted it, complicated it, and tried to add to it. When all is said and done, Howard, Jesus Christ is Lord."

I looked over at my roommate Dean. There was a moment of silence. Howard Be Thy Name looked over at me and asked, "Now what?" In a calm voice I asked Howard Be Thy Name, "Would you like to start life all over again, accepting God's grace to face your past and giving your life to Jesus Christ; accepting him as your personal Savior and Lord of your life?" Howard Be Thy Name, in a submissive, low voice, said, "Yes! I'm ready." Dean and I knelt with Howard Be Thy Name on our living-room floor and Howard Be Thy Name gave his life to Jesus Christ.

The weeks to follow were exciting. Howard Be Thy Name was reading his Bible, going to church, and sharing what he learned with Dean and me. His commitment and his changed life have encouraged me greatly. I shared Howard's decision with my seminary colleagues and the pastor of our church. I have no doubt that someday Howard Be Thy Name will be sharing with and bringing someone to the life-saving grace through faith in Jesus Christ.

Chapter 18
The Little Red Truck

I was sitting in a car on icy, snow-covered roads in a traffic jam. People were exiting an NFL football game between the Seattle Seahawks and the Denver Broncos. I should have been rejoicing over Seattle's win, but other things had taken my mind captive. As my friend Paul and I attempted to weave between cars on the icy roads, we noticed a little red truck stuck on the side of the road. We watched the driver rock the little red truck back and forth in an attempt to gain enough momentum to get over the hump of ice left by a snowplow. I noticed the little red truck had California license plates and obviously the driver wasn't used to driving on snow, let alone the glaze of ice that had covered the entire street.

In the fast pace of the bumper-to-bumper traffic jam, everyone was in a hurry to get home. They were paying little or no attention to the little red truck's dilemma. Paul encouraged me to hop out and give him a push. Paul left enough space for him to enter the flow of traffic in front of us. My weight pushing was just enough to get him over the hump. I couldn't have pushed him over the obstacle without him spinning his wheels and getting some traction, and he couldn't have made it on his own without that added little push I gave him. And it would have been futile to get the little red truck going without Paul leaving room for him to merge into traffic.

So often Christians forsake their Lord to drive on clear, dry roads in the world of carnality. Through whatever circumstances, we find ourselves back on the icy, slippery roads trying to live a spirit-filled life. We are foreigners to the trials—like, being from California and on an icy road—that we're not accustomed to. We rock back and forth, trying to get some traction, and just can't seem to make it over the icy bump of an obstacle. It doesn't take long for the Lord to send someone our way to give us that little push we need to get moving again. We find ourselves being pushed by words of encouragement from the Bible. This is what discipleship is all about. As the words of encouragement fill our spirits we get moving again. Once we're motivated, the family of God shares in our joy, and they stop the flow briefly to let us merge back into fellowship.

We are all called to be disciples of one sort or another. Mark, chapter 16, verse 20, tells us that disciples don't only share God's word; it states at the end of verse 20 that "his word was confirmed by signs that accompanied it." In other words our faith brings forth godly actions. What we do as disciples for Christ is provide the evidence for what we say.

If we as disciples pass an opportunity to share our Lord with those who are struggling, the blessing we could have will be passed on to someone else. A true disciple grows each time he or she takes on the task of encouraging others. Someday the pushee will become the pusher. That's when the true blessing of discipleship takes place. We stand back and watch the little red truck we once pushed pushing someone else.

Don't wait for the little red truck to ask for a push. Go and do it. He or she doesn't want to stay in one place, spinning their wheels. If they are spinning their wheels, they are willing to receive a push. Are you willing to leave the comfort of your nice, warm car and step out into the weather on the slippery road that your brother or sister in the Lord may be experiencing in an effort to return to fellowship with their Savior?

Chapter 19
After the Fact

A man's past can be a blessing to Christ, no matter how bad, how destructive, or how humiliating. It is through tragedy, sorrow, and affliction that God molds, builds, and strengthens his children. It grieves me, and I'm sure it grieves God, to hear another Christian talk about the tragedy of one's past as though it all should have been done differently. Remorseful statements after repentance such as, "If only I had done this!" or "If only they had not done that!" breed guilt. To repeat or hear again and again this type of statement does little to nourish a state of grace. In spite of me doing this and others doing that, God's grace through faith in Jesus Christ is all that matters after the fact. Could you imagine Christ, while he was dragging his cross to Calvary, looking at Peter and saying, "Oh, Peter, I wish you hadn't denied me three times," or perhaps giving Peter the famous line: "I knew it! I just knew it! You couldn't keep your mouth shut, could you?"

Part of our relationship with an all-knowing, all-forgiving, all-caring, and all-loving God is realizing that when we mess up, God still moves. He follows us, pursues us, and when our imperfect will reaches its end, he's there with his perfect will to forgive us, love us, encourage us, and restore us. It's the Holy Spirit's job to convict. It's the Christian's duty to plant seeds of forgiveness and restoration after the fact.

I remember a little bunny in a famous Walt Disney movie; his parents encouraged him not to discourage others. Thumper, in the movie *Bambi*, learned as a child, "If you can't say anything good, then don't say nothing at all." This lesson is also taught in Scripture in a somewhat different wording. James, chapter 3, verses 3 through 12, reads like this: "When we put bits into the mouths of horses to make them obey us, we can turn the whole animal. Or take ships as an example. Although they are so large and are driven by strong winds, they are steered by a very small rudder wherever the pilot wants to go. Likewise the tongue is a small part of the body, but it makes great boasts. Consider what a great forest is set on fire by a small spark. The tongue also is a fire, a world of evil among the parts of the body. It corrupts the whole person, sets the whole course of his life on fire, and is itself set on fire by hell. All kinds of animals, birds, reptiles and creatures of the sea are being tamed and have been tamed by man, but no man can tame the tongue. It is a restless evil, full of deadly poison. With the tongue we praise our Lord and Father, and with it we curse men, who have been made in God's likeness. Out of the same mouth come praise and cursing. My brothers, this should not be. Can both fresh water and salt water flow from the same spring? My brothers, can a fig tree bear olives, or a grapevine bear figs? Neither can a salt spring produce fresh water."

The final statement made by James in these verses sums it up: "Neither can a salt spring produce fresh water." Statements that don't encourage tend to discourage. I have witnessed the attitudes the words "If only" convey. They destroy people, families, churches, and the testimony of Jesus Christ. In conclusion, let us look at the past as an opportunity for ministry, a message of grace, covered by the blood and restorable by Almighty God himself.

Hindsight is better than 20/20 vision. It's covered by grace—after the fact.

Chapter 20

The Eyes of Grace

"Mr. Pilcher would like to speak with you, Dennis. Look, he's motioning for you to come over."

I looked across the dayroom and there sat an elderly man in a wheelchair. He could barely lift his arm and his hand was small, contorted, and feeble. As I walked over to the table to join this man, who desired my company, he kind of turned his head to the side and looked up at me. His eyes shone with an indescribable radiance, and his smile melted my heart. He reached out to shake my hand and all he could do was rest his hand in my open palm. Arthritis had taken its toll on the joints, and I could tell it hurt him just to have me touch his fingers, but he insisted.

"Hello, sir! My name is Dennis," I said. "You must be a minister," he answered. "Well, sir," I replied, "actually, I'm just getting started. I entered seminary three months ago." "Good for you!" he remarked. "I did the same thing eighty-two years ago, and my dad was a missionary. I'll be one hundred years old next month." It looked like everything had failed Mr. Pilcher except for his speech, his mind, and his eyesight. Mr. Pilcher's countenance stood out like that of the Jesus he had shared for the better part of a century.

I was doing my service and acquiring credit hours for a clinical pastoral education class. I had chosen this particular retirement center because I had visited it as an unsaved boy with my junior high youth group some twenty-three years before. I could have done my service in a prison, hospital, treatment center, or mental health ward. I chose the rest home because I had served as either a patient or an inmate in all the others. I was getting what I thought was a late start in my Lord's service. Mr. Pilcher told me I had plenty of time. He told me I could have fifty years if I kept myself fit and the Lord didn't call me home.

Although Mr. Pilcher and I were born sixty-three years apart, he described our lives as being interwoven. Mr. Pilcher had gone to Bible college within ten miles of where I was born in Geneva, New York. He had taught high school in Tacoma, Washington—the same district where I had attended, some 2,600 miles away from my place of birth. He also pastored a church in the same town, Battle Creek, Michigan, where God revealed his long-term plan for my life in the ministry.

God would bring Mr. Pilcher and me together in a retirement home that I had once attended as an unsaved eighth grader some twenty-three years earlier, to confirm his plan for me in the ministry.

I found myself fighting back the tears. I had worried that I had waited too long to answer my Lord's calling. Here was a seasoned pro telling me that I looked like a preacher. Mr. Pilcher also said that he could tell God was going to use me for a great ministry by the way I had spoken in the service earlier. This retirement home was a Christian center, and many of the married couples and single people who resided at this giant facility were retired preachers and missionaries. I was at the nursing home that adjoined the main facility. For most of the elderly there, that home was the final stop before eternity with their Lord.

I listened to the retired preacher as he shared stories of his days on the mission field just outside of Peking, China. I was blessed to hear about how God had spared him and his family numerous times from the warlords who ran rampant through China in the early 1900s.

"One time," he reported, "I ducked behind a large rock after a hail of gunfire. I checked on my six-month-old son, whom I had been carrying in a crude, wooden-type cradle. As I pulled the blankets away, I found a bullet underneath the bedding. The Lord had protected and spared my son."

He shared this like it had happened just the day before. He finished his sharing with this statement: "So hang in there, Dennis; it can only get better."

That night I shared with my Lord what a wonderful time I had spent with my new friend. Many thoughts, all of which were peaceful and pleasant, passed through my mind. It dawned on me that I hadn't chosen that retirement facility. Actually, it had been on my mind for weeks. The Holy Spirit knew I would be meeting and talking to my predecessor.

God was showing me what life and his purpose in my life was all about. The Lord had sent me the closest thing to an angel he had in his service. Mr. Pilcher didn't know about the trials in my life, but he spoke as if he did. His focus was on my perseverance in the ministry and for my Lord. Mr. Pilcher couldn't write anymore, so I wrote for him in the front of my Bible, "So hang in there, Dennis; it can only get better!" And I signed it "Jesus." I fell asleep that night seeing in Mr. Pilcher's eyes the peace, the love, and the beauty of eternity just around the corner.

The next time I see eyes anything like Mr. Pilcher's, I will be face-to-face with my Lord and Savior Jesus Christ.

Conclusion

I look at a man like myself and think, *There is no one like me. I am one of a kind.* After all, how many men have been through what I have? The variety of tragedy is astounding to me, now that I look back on it. Every day I look at what God has done inside me. It is evident to others, as is every garment designed by Jesus Christ.

Consider the centurion who was astounded by what took place at Calvary and said, "Truly this man was the Son of God." He witnessed God's predesigned pattern become a reality through the tragedy of the Crucifixion. He was witnessing the birth pains of grace.

Only a seamstress can take abstract material and lace, visualize, and then make a beautiful, country-style dress. Only the Holy Spirit, through a man's faith in Jesus Christ, can take inconsistencies, tragedies, and strife and sew together *a Garment of Grace*.

A Final Thought

I never imagined the dedication, thought, and the amount of people it took to bring into completion just one small book. We all walk into libraries and look for information, or pick out a good book, and take for granted the great investment made in the finished product. Each one of us is a book: an eternal being, the product of an investment of grace. I think of the time and patience God is using to bring us all to completion. Each of us will walk into heaven someday and see the greatest library of all. The books of renown will be the ones that didn't sit around and collect dust. This has been quite an adventure, the investment great, the pain indescribable. I suppose that is the cost of anything worth writing about. Someday I will talk to the writer of the greatest Book of all; the number-one seller yesterday, today, and forever. 'Tis then I'll meet the author face to face.